The Word for Everything

Roger Mitchell

BkMk Press

THE UNIVERSITY OF MISSOURI–KANSAS CITY

The author would like to thank the editors of the following journals where some of these poems first appeared: *Amicus Journal, Antioch Review, Crazyhorse, Denver Quarterly, Flying Island, Hopewell Review, New England Review, The Ohio Review, Passages North, Ploughshares, Poetry, Poetry Northwest, Puerto del Sol, Spoon River Poetry Review.*

"Strong Coffee" first appeared in *The Jazz Poetry Anthology: Second Set,* edited by Sascha Feinstein and Yusef Komunyakaa.

A special thanks to Ragdale art colony where many of these poems were either written or polished and to my wife, Dorian Gossy, who gave this book numerous helpful readings. Thanks, too, to the members of two workshops I was a part of, one in 1986 (Dean Young, Lynda Hull, David Wojahn, Jim Harms, Yusef Komunyakaa), and the other for about three years in the early nineties (Alice Friman, Elizabeth Krajeck, Catherine Swanson, Tam Neville, Bert Stern, Dick Pflum, Roger Pfingston, Tom Koontz, Haven Koontz, Bonnie Maurer).

Financial assistance for this book has been provided by the Missouri Arts Council, a state agency.

Book design by Sherry Sullivan
Cover design by Brad Kelley. E-mail: coolgrafix@gvi.net;
Web: http://home.gvi.net/~coolgrafix/
Cover photograph by Dorian Gossy

Library of Congress Cataloging-in-Publication Data

Mitchell, Roger, -
    The word for everything / Roger Mitchell.
        p.   cm.
    ISBN 1-886157-06-5
    I. Title.
PS3563.I82W7   1996
811'.54—dc20   96-22242
                                                         CIP

Other Books by Roger Mitchell

Poetry
Letters from Siberia and Other Poems
Moving
A Clear Space on a Cold Day
Adirondack

Non-Fiction
Clear Pond: The Reconstruction of a Life

Contents

To Dorian

and to the memory of my father

("Put calla by the willow")

The Word for Everything

You're Here

and despite all the tricks of dis-
placement and slid syntax,
despite all you know of the need
the mind has to be elsewhere,
or the greased border between world
and the words that would say they
were the world, you know where you are.
I know. I should be talking
in images. I should be over there.
But I'm here, and though it's a place
with a name and a kind of look
to the hills and the way rocks
break through the skin of the earth
exposing the bones,
and the people seem relentless,
I can still stand at the corner
of First and Woodlawn and feel
what I've always felt, at all
the corners: a part of the wind.
The wind that right now at the end
of August refuses to move,
that last year snapped the Lombardy poplar,
that carries the ash and the dust,
that brings the sighs and the sirens,
the curses, right into the living room,
last repository and resting place
for all the last words and the last
strangled breathings, that must be,

or enter, the birds' anatomy,
that must be, or resemble, a sea,
or the currents of that sea,
in which we do, if we do,
the singular swim, the long
slippery lope, of being here.

Loon

We went out upon the lake,
quietly. In a canoe,
we went out. Not very far,
as it was getting dark,
but we went out
and crept along the shore.
Slowly and without talking,
we went out.
And without lifting the paddle
from the water,
so that there would not be
even the sound of dripping
when we went out.
And there was nothing in that silence
but itself.
Invisible twitters
in the underbrush,
plus whatever sound it is
the air makes
rubbing against itself.
Maybe there will be a loon tonight, we said.
There wasn't,
but we went out anyway
into a sort of inhabited silence,
at dusk, with pink light fading
and one bird
perched in the top limb of a dead tree.
It flew, and the sky
was several colors of dark blue slate,

and the lily pads
from which the lilies
recently had fallen,
rested on the water.
We had been in that tiny bay
the year before, also at dusk.
The sky had been dramatic then, impending,
streaked vermilion and blue.
Now it was slate blue and gray,
but changing, changing fast.
This year is like the last, we said,
but different.
We were as we were, as well,
though changed.
It was dusk and the end of summer
and the lake was probably dying,
though you could not tell it,
and we paddled back to the dock
as though we had heard a call,
as though before we would even see it,
whatever it might be
would dive and disappear.

Borrowing Henry

The little essay on the ant creeps forth
on the assumption that someone—Jim, let us say—
listens. Jim is not obliged to listen,
and to judge from the blank days in the journal
and the perfectly wooden passages,
which Henry, of course, would think improved
for resembling the xylem and phloem,
Jim wanders off at times, no one knows where.
Jim is the reason Henry hurries back
from Conantum. Jim is the reason
he sits up late with a candle or lamp
and thinks about two hawks. Jim, he would say,
and he would tell him something odd. And Jim
would say, "That's odd," the way Henry wanted,
or Jim might nod or gaze at the ceiling.
And Henry, remembering each detail,
would tell how the tightly compacted fawn
falls out of its mother, almost like shitting,
the nose pressed down between the two front feet,
the doe twisting to get her body right
and tossing her head back to look, sniffing
the new birth. This, he would say, and then stop.
He would think of the smell of the body.
Jim, he would say. But Jim would be gone by then.
It was a marvel. He could be right there
in his room thinking, Jim in the corner,
the lamp filled and the wick trimmed down.
Then he'd be gone, into the body, say,
into the body of a doe, his nose

pressed flat between his hands, a terrible
convulsion thrusting at him, squeezing him,
and when he thought his ribs would crack, and the whole
sky shove into his chest at once, the air
licked him, stood shaken above him, sniffing.

Clang

A woman stands in a cornfield at the end of day.
Nowhere does the "extensive totality of life"
bear down with such menace as in southern Indiana.
These are not just rocks by the side of the road.
It is not just a pleasantness of trees
that gathers here. The man out back
raises a maul above his head and brings it down
with enough force to change the course of a life.
It is the straight green grain of black locust,
and like a good life it sings when it's split.

The leaves come down off the trees in the fall,
and there's a moment near dusk when you don't know
if it's the last of the swifts racing
for its hole or the first uncertain bat
launching its night-long raid on the bug life,
which may be the true life, of this wrinkled
republic, this land careening down a hill
of river bottoms, ox bows, limestone and mud.

Music I Knew

It was in Katowice, I think, in Silesia,
where the Polish border officials
in their snug uniforms of olive brown
boarded the trains going south into Czechoslovakia.
We were swarmed over in minutes by gypsies
going home for Christmas, assuming
that gypsies have a home, and Christmas.
Each year at that time those from the mines
and factories of southern Poland
go south into Czechoslovakia, and on,
I was told, into Hungary where gypsies,
briefly, cease being themselves and settle down.

Across from me the woman with no teeth
and black shining eyes had seven skirts
which she lifted like a bundle of laundry,
an armful of curtains, in search of a passport,
when the smiling border official slammed
the glass door back and shouted in seven languages
at once, none of them gypsy, "Passports, please."
Mine lay on my lap, the blank page turned.
The little gypsy girl, who also had seven skirts,
each for a time in her life when she would cease
being the person she was and start
being someone else, dodged among them
with a plastic bag full of passports,
collecting and dispensing at random,
to all her brothers and sisters, to all
her mothers and fathers, one jump ahead

of the trim border officials whose duty
to protect the state from disorder is hard,
who keep their minds on their high, clear task
and stamp with a small spring-loaded stamp,
eventually, whatever is laid before them.

I think it was that night, later,
after the gypsies had risen at Prague
in a body and burrowed into the darkness,
steam swirling along the platforms,
in search of a train that would take them
back into Hungary. Though who would have room
in Hungary to house these hundreds, with their skirts
and their bags full of fresh kohlrabi,
which they cut with a wide-bladed knife
on the thick flat pad of their thumbs
and eat in the same closed compartment as you
offering you some, too, which you take
and say, thank you, I come from America,
I live in a house, the night is cold.

It was then, that night,
when the gypsies were gone, when the spunk
and the sharp smell of kohlrabi stayed on
with the long sinews of tribes and the songs,
which we have only learned to disguise,
as we crept toward Vienna and Rome,
that the family from somewhere in central Europe got on.
And all night, as we rattled south toward the border
or waited, murmuring, on unlit sidings,
were slammed out of something like sleep
by several smiling officials, as our passports

were looked at and stamped and looked at again,
I watched, in the dim light, under the lid of sleep,
the mother, the father, two daughters, a son,
drink something clear from each other's glances.

It was a hot, cramped compartment on a train
crossing central Europe twenty years ago.
It was a night full of slammed doors and songs
sung in the back of my throat, as I slept
or pretended to sleep, as I crept forward
toward Vienna and Rome, the rest of my life,
listening to a music I had never heard, but knew,
a song I would come to sing, already mine.

Remember

I remember going somewhere in a car.
Black shadows gathered
under some trees. That was the way
things happened then. Afternoon.
A large house by a lake.

It must have been Lake George.
Up the west side somewhere near
Bolton Landing. I don't know why
I know that. We were there
for the afternoon, I don't know

why or for how long. I just remember
shadows milking the trees,
the brooding of a large house
at the edge of them, and beyond it,
a shimmer of water.

I go back to this memory
from time to time, wondering
what it was, whether anything other
than shadows and a large house
beside a lake brought us there,

wondering what, if anything,
happened, and why, whether anyone
remembers why shadows gathered

and fell, sank into the ground,
whether anyone remembers anything.

What did that afternoon belong to?
To us? The memory of us?
What were the shadows and the trees,
and we, gathered there to do?
I was too small to know, four or five.

Yet I am the one still there,
standing by the lake and the dark hovering
next to it, the house I recall
nothing of but its wide summer porches,
and the watery lake beside it.

Maybe something in the word beside.
Maybe the heaviness of the trees.
It was closer to me, I suppose,
than the others, whoever
the others were, and made me see

the darkness, that it grew
next to houses, and above them,
that you could be beside a house
and in it, that you could pull
black trees around you, and the lake.

That all of this would disappear,
the reason and the people, the house,
but the darkness and the lake

would not, that we would become
these things, that we were already,

that it would take a lifetime
to find and find a way to say it,
saying darkness to the trees,
shimmer to the lake, saying
somewhere, or, remember.

Rendered World

He walks down into a field
at the beginning of winter
to look at the marks on a stone.
Everything is dead.
The deer have brushed the grasses aside
like waves for their bowers.
The markings are little markings,
veins in a filament.
The branches of the trees quiver,
the sky boils. It is the time
when only the ground is full,
a pudding of slick muds.
The chickadees are furious
about everything, especially
about everything.
The hawk backs off and waits.
The man is down here trying
to fold a leaf into a bird,
a bird into a hidden cloud,
without being seen.
He knows he is not alone,
yet he can't quite get his arm
around the box elder, the hawk
backing away, the twists of bleached
grasses pushed into layered
arabesques by the haunches
of sleeping deer, the wind twanging
the stalks of dead weeds,
the world rendered to its

red-brown browns, its grays, its
stripped limbs, chickadees and crows,
its quaking, fertile understuff,
its mud, its various muds, the muds
of weeds, of beds of grasses,
moss muds and ruddy muds,
muds you could paint with, muds
you could smear over the body,
blood muds and muds you could
bake into bricks or, with straw,
into doorstops, paperweights,
into unformed lumps, primary
and dropped, graven and silent.
For what is it can stand
next to this deep bleakness
but itself.

Old Summer

It was hot and it was night
and the dresser with glass knobs glowed.
It was time to lie down,
time to look back at the wall
and the wallpaper stuck to the wall.
The violin drifted up from the restaurant
by the beach. The ocean rubbed it raw.
I thought of the lucky eaters,
knives beside their plates.
Forty years later the restaurant
burned to the ground. The violin wavered
again. I thought of the silence
down at the water's edge.
They could call you and call you,
and you couldn't hear.
I call and call, and what do you hear,
thin violin, unbreakable beach?

Sneaking Out at Night

The sun seeps through a ruffled veil of cloud,
making a white like old ice on skating rinks
in remote mountains. One night I snuck out
with my skates and whisked across the lake
toward the dust of lights on the far shore.
It was the lights I went for, but the lake
stayed with me. Out in the middle, the dark
drew in. The wind made spaces in the hum
that filled my body then. Out on the thin
skin of the water, invisible, I stopped.

Or I stop now. Then I was someone else
and did not stop. And there was someone
with me. A boy. We were both boys, and he—
and I suppose we both knew this might happen—
has disappeared from my life, as I nearly have
myself. Two boys, friends in a way, dashing
across black water in the dark.

Return to a Small Town

It is and isn't there. The movie house
erased by grass, the lives I used to live
replaced by others, or not replaced.
I look for names on signs, flip standing up
at a pay phone through rain-rumpled pages,
though it wasn't names I memorized, but cracks
in sidewalks, looks on passing faces.
Nothing fits the two aging women
(both of whom I may have danced with in the gym)
standing by the city's cement planter, talking
about someone's heart. Or the man thumbing his wrist
(the bulging vein pops quickly back in place)
behind the register. I agree. It's hot
and no one's buying. He puts the T-shirt
in a bag, folds it, stops, folds it again.
He doesn't hear me say, I came from here.
Or does. Maybe that's what rummaging
among the day's receipts means. Maybe
that's what saying nothing says,
looking across the sagging racks of shirts
that no one wants, even at half price.

The Glass on the Table

I have not found the word for the way
the glass is on the table,
but it is there. It is also morning,
and though it is a thousand miles away,
I am trying to think of the ocean.
When I go down to it now,
I walk out past the waves
to the place where the waves begin.
Or seem to begin. Where the water heaves
a little and then subsides,
has an idea and then thinks better of it.
There must be an explanation for this.
Someday I will go there and know why
I let the water lift me up
and set me down, rock me
in its cradle. It was this,
I remember, or something like it,
that made me think of jellyfish.
Though that isn't the word, exactly.
There is no word, of course,
for anything. The glass on the table
may be empty, but it is also full.

Fantasia, with John Locke

. . . to sit down in a quiet ignorance of those Things, which,
upon Examination, are found to be beyond the reach of our
Capacities.

John Locke

To sit down in a quiet ignorance, John.
To sit down on this slow, rolling dune
in a wind that will not end. In December,
to sit down among things, scrub oak
and the flittering black-tipped wings,
things that roll over the blown grass, John,
beyond, as you say, the reach of our capacities,
grass and the rib of blackened sand
that cuts across this gigantic eye-bowl
like a slit in a mask, paths which start
and end in the same arbitrary swale,
the clouds, far off, urging themselves onward,
the boisterous waves bowing to the sand
in this last and first place, this wind,
this sun like hard, blue glass, to sit down,
blazing with emptiness, by the jack pine
and the may bush and the perfect circles
off the compass grass, to sit down, the reach
of our capacities, for the moment, reached,
the rest let go.

Once Upon a Time

I liked the lies I told you of the wolves
the best, I think. The wolves were always kind.
They took you off, but always brought you back.
Two little girls who lived in a small cabin
at the edge of a dark woods. They were brave.
When the great wolf scratched at the door, they went,
stopping only to see that the goat was tied.
The parents grieved when the children disappeared,
but not for long. The hay had to be cut
and the table scrubbed. The sun would soon set,
and winter was near. Nearby, a mother died,
and the father hung himself in the barn.
It was part of the story. It had to be told.
When the wolf scratched at the door, the mother
opened one eye. The father forgot to breathe.
They lay in the dark and listened to it,
till the first light cracked and the rooster crowed
and the sun said, now.
                                        Once upon a time,
the story started. Once upon a time,
it said. At the edge of a deep, dark forest,
a deep, dark thing took place.

What Happens Next

We don't know what happens next in John Sloan's
5 x 7 etching, "Man, Wife and Child."
The man's suspenders dangle off his back.
Plump and still corseted, the wife leans
into him. And he leans back. They stand, hugging
each other hugely, holding the other's eyes
with a fond, playful lust which the child, dressed
in a loose jumper for bed, her head too large
for her body, her thoughts starting to beat
like a startled wren against the dresser, the chair,
the small framed print, the broad-bellied pitcher
in its bowl, finds almost wonderful.
She reaches out as if to join their dance,
a dance she almost knows the music to.
But these two upright wrestlers (the wife pulls—
she may be merely hanging on—at the back
of his collarless shirt opening) don't know,
for the moment, she's there, don't care. Though, of course,
they do. They live in a room together,
and the stiff collar stands like a sentinel
on the dresser, the tie, untied, still threaded
through it. Drawers stand open, a spoon slants
out of a cup, or is it a bowl, and the girl,
who came from something like this, and almost knows it,
who ought to be in bed, but isn't, sees
that tonight it doesn't matter, and won't
ever again. Her mother's forearm grips
the small of her father's back. It's 1905.
What happens next is nothing next to this.

Mobile Homes

It's like the bird I saw off in the distance
yesterday, black with the long, watery flap
crows have in flight. There was no one with me
in the car, but I said it anyway "Crow."
Or, standing in the checkout line later—
a half gallon of milk and a loaf of bread—
the man with the loaded cart said, "You go first."
You drive into town past the largest lots
of mobile homes you ever saw, and the road
goes over a creek or a railroad track,
and there they are again, behind a tangle
of some bush I don't know the name of—twelve
dozen or so—lived in a little too long,
so close together you can hardly breathe.
I've gotten to the point where I can see
a thing at a distance, like a bird, or clouds,
like dirt by the side of the road, and not
be too surprised when it starts becoming
mobile homes. They call them that, and they may be,
but the people in them seem stuck,
and not just next to a stinkwater creek
forever, a battering all-night highway.
It's important to think things matter,
since they may not. I spend more of my time now
driving. Highways are just long places.
It's the fields I look out into, the fields
that seem to go on for a while and stop.
Like the one with the county home in it.
The windows are smashed and something like
"Help Deth" scrawled there. Death, who needs no help.

City of Back Yards

A sprinkle of ash on the lip of the wood stove
like a burped baby. This is the only place I've lived
long enough to have burnt the fence.
Here the rug lies down like an old dog
and the unwashed light piles up in the corner .

No one I knew ever lived here. None
ever drove through. I stick my seeds in the ground
each spring and cut down a wiry assortment
of grasses, wildflowers, ground ivies and weeds
to keep it from disappearing.
I know the cracks in my sidewalk exactly,
which root of which tree passed through,
the place where the water slipped in one March.

The alleys threaded through this town,
worms in an odd compost,
end in a tumbled wall or rotting garage.
Poles sizzle on summer nights
lugging their tonnage of volts
to the wheezing air-conditioners.
This is where garbage and cars
and the weekend gardens,
the half-built seesaws and broken lamps,
shoe boxes full of old letters,
albums of forgotten friends,
are put on display for the curious rain.

I look at the staid, plain houses
of the people who lived here once,
the brick stacked up in its bricky way,
the wooden lintels, the back doors snug in their jambs.
Forget-me-nots cluster in the shadows of stumps.
Unleashed forsythia bounds up from the grass
for the twelfth time, thirty feet away.
And here, seven mail boxes
are nailed above the broken doorbell.
Seven samples of soap are newly placed there,
seven gestures of hope.

Strong Coffee

Strong coffee going upstream, slow jazz
coming down. Unmistakable Milt Jackson,
the sun translucing his cool vibrato.
Praise John Lewis, that philosopher of the
interval, the one between the meaning and
the meaning, slow to break open the chord,
tireless in working out the calculus
of feeling. You come away loosened a little
along the fault line between the coastal
shelf you came from, waving its sinuous
underwater weed, and the crumbling range
of dust and hill you built your life on,
incipient mud slide, that cactus ranch
of choices made in the name of what
somebody's mother knew well led to hell's
spectacularly barnacled foyer. Oh yes,
whoever she was, she made it possible,
over and over, to be lifted. She brought
Johnny Hodges directly up out of the
bloodstream, stroking his velvet sax.
I learned my mambo because she knew,
but would not say, where it would lead.
But it led there, straight as whiskey
in a straw. I thank my mambo for what
she taught me with her silence. So what
if I got there just as the band broke out
in "Fugazzi's Blues." I got there.

Seeing Some Feral Goats

There was a fence, a loosened
strand of hair, and so
something of a kept
appearance to the place.
And half way down to the sea
the winding one-track road
or worn way over the two-
hundred-year-old boil and spill
of dark metallic lava,
out of which wild lantana
and half domestic zinnia sprang,
wound past the thrown-back limbs
of a single dead kiawe,
thrown back no doubt by the wind,
but thrown over crumbled walls,
the shade of someone gone
(the shade, too, gone)
who daily looked down
the long slope to the sea,
at the grassy intervals and rock,
the sea breaking soundlessly.
Above us, then, we saw,
or heard before we saw,
six lava-colored goats
and a seventh, almost white,
who, when they saw us, ran
clattering across the rocks,
though all we did was stop
and look up, ran

as though they knew,
and would have told us what,
but for a quickness in the legs.
And though the last rust-
blackened runt stopped
to look back, before
rattling on into the next
ashen valley, clinkered
meadow, they were not calm,
as I assume they came to be,
until they'd disappeared.
There, where almost nothing grew
and no one lived, or,
till now, thought to.

North

I had been watching them drift up and down
the channel for an hour, trying to see
against gray cloud and failing light what sort
of thing it was that moved like confetti,
blowing trash above a landfill, snow.
They drove upstream, beating in slow
somnolent strokes, then came back, beating
in the same persistent way. I listened.
It may have been wind, but I don't remember
their cries. Though they must have cried. To themselves, at least.
One of them banked steeply and dropped a wing
into the water, just the tip. Another, the same.
They were here, certainly, but not for long.
You could see it the way they came down at last,
in twos and threes, packing together tightly,
stepping, it seemed, almost reluctantly
into the water. They did this three times, each time
exploding upward into vague barreling
formations, then falling slowly to the water,
and always aimed, all of them, the same way.
North, as I now realize.
      The last time,
when the rolling swirl seemed to move upward,
when it was sky they wanted, and more sky,
I had to squint to keep from losing them.
The clouds kept shoving to the east, layer
on smudged layer, dragging the light with it.
At last I could see them only through glass
and only when they banked their darker gray

against the one that crept crazily
along the shore, the rocks, the trees fallen
face first into the water, and the water.
And then, as if on a blind cue, the swirl
collapsed, and a wedge, almost a wing,
assembled itself from the scattered flecks.

I'm not sure what happened next, after the thing
swung slowly around, headed the wrong way.
By then I knew that everything I'd seen,
even the drifting up and down, was part
of the one thing, undertow and tide
and the dragging sand. They turned, of course.
It was the way they turned, the way things turn
that are difficult. Ungraceful, slow,
appearing to lose purpose and direction,
liable to reversion, tentative.
But go, finally, the way they were meant to,
though they were kept from knowing what it would be.

Segments of Spine

A squashed bottle or torn bag
ground into the cinders by the roadside,
volcanic dust. We had come down the west
side of the island, through eucalyptus
and long-needled pine. The road
rolled over thick tendons of mountain,
the potholes and rocks loosening the car
from its own bolts. We turned east
onto a slope of old lava, black
and rust red, the scorch of original earth.
Spiked bushes in clusters, cactus,
the odd kiawe twisted up out of rock,
the occasional breath of a meadow—
a lung among all those bones—the sea
blue-purple and green beyond, wind stretched
tight across its belly. We parked the car,
a banged-up, off-white rental, the kind
now and again pushed into the guavas,
under the monkey pods, the hanging trumpets.
Or like the one we saw completely beached
on the rocks, stripped and beaten to a thin
skeleton of rust. We got out and stood
looking, now at the ground, the crushed bottle
or torn bag in the cinders, now downhill,
the mile or two it was to the coast, the six
or so it was beyond where sea
turned to sky. But it was up into the rock
ravines we looked longest, arroyos, deep

creases in the slopes, which if your eye kept
climbing, took you up declivities
you could only imagine, ledges even
the goats avoided, birds circled warily,
where mountain stopped and the flat underside
of cloud began. Later, we would come upon bones
in a small grove of kukui, lumbar
arrangements, pelvic scoops, scattered
segments of spine. Though I remember
the pig-shaped swarm of maggots laid
in the toothed shadow of a palm.
And once, clambering up a ridge,
startling the black, bearded billy of all
these gullies and his two current consorts,
one of whom, dragging a back leg, stumbled
and fell as they scrambled to get away,
stumbled again, stopped, and stood staring
at the rock in front of her. It seemed then
she might decide this was the place, the way
when the lion in the film finally
brings the Thompson's gazelle down, and before
its teeth meet each other in the neck,
the gazelle has gone to sleep. All day we climbed,
not caring where the folds in the landscape
took us. Once, through a maze of kiawe,
out onto rock ledges scored by the goats,
we came into a grove of thready limbs.
Two low caves thrust into a wall—
a cul-de-sac—of rock, reeking of cat,
fetor of pig. Clambering, we came out
onto the grazed bend in a ridge and stopped,

the wind carrying a small whinny down
from the cloudy portages above us.

I don't quite know what it means, if it means
anything, to climb down into the skull
of a dry creek, to run your hands along
the smoothed outer curve of water.
Cloud comes down and calm ravages the air.
We want to be where we are, but we can't
quite find it. You shout from the other side
of a ridge. You have almost broken loose,
gone past, but at the last possible gasp
of immensity, pull back, your face pale.
I want to go up into the cloud, you say,
but I want you to go with me.

Four Hundredth Mile

I am 83 miles north of Indianapolis on I-65.
A few clouds are out and the corn stands
dead on its feet on either side of the road.
It is dusk and the light leaps up
to take its last look at the world.
It is September, early September, and the leaves,
though they feel the soft stroking of the air,
shiver slightly.
I am driving my four hundredth mile of the day,
alone now, and calm, the lights of the oncoming cars
beginning to sparkle in the dying light.
Huge flat-sided semis, as the night comes on,
pass like immense untroubled animals,
like the sides of houses in a flood.
How many times have I been here and not seen
the width of the sky, the slow curve of the landscape
going away, the tiny wire trailing after?

This is the place and this, undoubtedly, the way.
As much of the sky above as there can be,
as much of the earth beneath.
This is the place where the world appears
in its robe of night and day,
where the dirt road travels with us a ways
and then turns sharply along the ditch,
disappearing down interminable rows of corn.
This is the place where you can see forever,
where pure emptiness hangs on outspread wings
circling above a field.

The soul ranges everywhere and everywhere finds
what it needs, a stick, a fleck of matter on the tongue.
The bird at the top of the dead tree will fly
before I can see it, so I will see it fly.
The cow in the truckbed in front of me looks out
at the world and, if I'm not mistaken, sees it.
The car makes a steady wind-ripped thrum, the glow
of the dashboard rising into my eyes like dust.
I am somewhere between exits. The promising sign,
"Vacancy," flashes above trees in the distance.
I am in no hurry. The only thing in front of me
is home, a few stars, and another night.
I have tried to love what I thought was the world,
but the world moved. I will love the move instead.

The Word for Everything

There is the word for you
and beside it the word *me*,
though neither of us knows which they are.
There is the word for the two of us, together
or apart. Together
and apart.
There is the word for chair,
the word *clear*.

There is the word for this moment, too,
though no one can pronounce it.
It is not now,
though there is the word *now*,
and the word *slow*.
Between them is the word
one does not hear,
the word these words look for,

here by the clear chair
deep in the slow now.

Old Road

Those who had this place picked for them stand
in the doorways of small white houses and look
back at you, drink whiskey in the graveyards
late at night and throw their empties
at the stones, some with their own names
already carved there. That's the fantasy,
at least. These are the ones who took what was there,
stayed put. I come along on a stray day,
driving, trying to get my mind around
a bend, not lost, but a stranger to this place.
The woman in the seat beside me asks
if we can't stop, if we can't get out
and walk along the road. It's an old road,
one that imitates the creek beside it,
turns where it turns, doubles back. We are trying
to make our minds up, not just about the future,
but about hills, the way they rise and fall,
the way they walk off blindly into trees
or sky, the way grass or something like it
grows everywhere, crowds down onto the road
where we walk beside one another
and sink our minds slowly into themselves,
into the fields, the woods, the box elder,
where the whole well-formed hind leg of a dog
sticks up out of its carcass, no longer
distinguishable from the weeds, leaf rot
and scattered refuse there, and the catbird
caterwauls in the multiflora rose,
now clawing its ravenous blooms outward,

its blooms portending everything at once.
We don't quite see it at the time, but this
is the place where it happens. We don't quite
know what it is, either, whether it's the car
tilted like a toy at the field's edge,
the field itself, a carpet thrown across
a hill, the bug drone, sink hole, barkless tree,
the long-haired shirtless boys who pass us twice
in a growling, high-backed Pontiac Grand Am,
the old man in the village with a stick,
struggling up his lawn, the front porch flush
to the ground, the life that is so much itself
it bursts like a bloated possum, a skunk
that leaves its dying on the air for days.
We dream it down to the carved bouquet
on a stone, to a single finger pointing
at a cloud, to four crows passing overhead.

Driving, Some Used Cars

I gave the gas a little extra pedal,
and with a mounting smooth metallic hum,
the car responded, cutting a wide arc
around the laggard Honda Civic, somewhat
battered and rust-embroidered. I was fresh
from running and a shower, hair still damp,
eye, hand, and mirror fused, and making calm,
accurate and instantaneous
adjustments at high speed with death buckled
in the seat beside me coolly measuring
the force at impact of bone on dashboard
at various illegal rates of speed.
I was at ease, breaking only a little
the law no one else seemed to have heard of.
Which tape of myself would I play that night?
Would I be anxious as I ate crawfish
with old friends soon to leave for California?
Would I be thoughtful, outrageous, both?
Would I make small talk with an undertone
of ominous panache? Fold sugar bags?
I would not know how to eat crawfish
(and so be saved disabling choices),
but shown the way, soon crunched, dismantled, licked
like any alligator in a swamp.
We ate and were distracted, he by a lost
contact lens, she by the daily made-up
nature of things. Would California be
there when they got down from their smoking Volvo
(source of many jokes)? Unbearable,

the last long day, coming in from Reno,
the temperature ninety-three, odor
of dust and oil, sweat and transpierced air,
whiff of Pacific spume reaching them
as coastal valleys open and descend.

It was my car and I was driving it.
I thought of it as mine. I think of it
as mine, as I do my life, which of course
isn't very much, but is what I am
or am doing or carrying around,
inventing, dropping, picking up, forgetting,
pushing up and down the freeways in one
or another of several wheeled conveyances,
metallic, self-propelling. Life is strange.
I was changing lanes (the car propelled,
in fact, by gas, the pedal, me, a piece
of what I earn), looking both front and back
as the spurt pushed me past the banged Honda,
and for the briefest clap of time, I saw
the old woman driving it, the story
she had told herself, apartment somewhere,
people waved to, a robe she wore at night,
dishes put away, cats fed, a gratitude
of things accomplished, things still to be done.
A list, maybe. Three small cups in a row.

It's a small car, red, used, just the right size
for changing lanes quickly, getting down
the road, thinking of things just beyond
the reach of what you call, because you have
no other word for it, life. For a moment,

yesterday afternoon, I was there,
abreast and gaining, neither leaning out
over sombre evening, looking for an end
to come to, nor a child back chopping
to free some plausible, vine-strangled morning.

Accident Report

Doris, whose glasses ride underslung
temples, whose wrists cut intricate
flicks, sack-bellied Boyle and suave
Petrocelli, black-maned and thick-
waisted, for all of whom the counter
is a sand-bagged bunker, an Alamo
of clipboards, handcuffs, CB monitors,
the woman handcuffed to the wall
in the back room ("Is she sleeping?"
"No, she's under arrest."), the pimp
in the purple beret who may be doing
undercover, too, the man who's been told
to go, that he's not done anything
anyone would spend the money to prove
("It's a gift," says Boyle, "take it.")
but doesn't believe it, the grit
ground into the floor tiles, cracks
in the glass on top of the one desk,
and Petrocelli's sleek leather boots
that lie there like sleeping lizards,
one across the other, and Boyle
whose sister's a Sister Something
I can't make out above Doris insisting
it had to have numbers ("Without
an address, we do not have an accident.").
She snaps the pencil down on the counter
and steps away. This is the third time
she's had it today. And the tired woman
in the rose coat that's seen the slope

of too many shoulders, smoking in what
you'd call on another block the foyer,
locked in that cubicle of gray light
like a bug in amber, staring at the near
face of the glass, at the x-ray taken
of her last ten years. It's not that
nobody knows she's there. It's the kid
in the torn T-shirt and the smell
of burnt coffee, hours under the glare
of heartburn, the hiss of styrofoam.
It's the coming down to the ground floor
fast. It's wishing you'd sent the check
or stayed home or tried to make it stick
or not said what you said in 1972.
I think of the man who couldn't
believe it. I can hardly believe it
myself. It may not have a fixed address
or a face. You may not know the model
or make. Maybe it didn't see you. Maybe
you weren't there. Maybe you got away
with something, your life, say, the next
twenty minutes. Was there a witness?
What happened, exactly? Did it happen
to you? How do you know? Is it happening
now? Is it still happening now?

Rubble

What good does it do to show us the picture
of the woman in Beirut with her hand to her face?
Who cares if the child is not hers, if the look
on her face is a look we have seen before,
that her dress doesn't fit and her hair's a mess?
Should we want to look at the body of the child
any more than she, at the foot with the shoe still tied,
at the sheet of bent cardboard laid hastily over it?
Whose side should we be on, the side of the child,
the side of the shoe still tied, the side of the rubble?
The rubble, at least, can't bleed.
It can't hold its hand in front of its face.
It can't twist its mouth like a torn lily, or think,
maybe it was a mistake for the first fish
to thrash up the first beach looking for air.
Or maybe we shouldn't have worlds. Maybe
we should have rubble instead, nothing but rubble.

Spring Wind

Yes, the shadows do seem to sprinkle
like first rain when the wind wakes the tops
of the cottonwoods far down the meadow.
And yes, you could say the leaves jitter,
jitter lazily, as the wind combs through them.
The bolls of the cottonwoods blowing, too,
billow as though we were underwater,
and the deep rocking of the branches
underneath the leaves, rocking from the trunk,
rocking from the ground itself, lulls us, yes.
You could say the earth was in a rush,
a kind of slow rush, everything leaning
or whispering, making a kind of speech
you cannot entirely hear, or decipher.
You could say these things, and more. You could say
what the wind says, yes, and the leaves say, too.

Wreck

1

My father finally had the wreck last week
that told him what was what. His lip is cut,
and if you listen hard you hear the leak
in the word "fine" as he works to get it out.
"I'm vine," he says, mouthing the new stitches.
Though there's so much wire between us, it might
be that. Do they still send these messages
that way, or do they bounce them off the light?
The moon looks adamant tonight, though why
I can't say, since when I hear my father
on the other side of things, I wonder
where we are. I know, of course. The sky
is lying in my lap. It's just that now
I wish for less clarity somehow.

2

And if you listen hard, the leak you hear
is father. He struggles to get it out.
It's the word "fine" that finally the ear
wrecks against. What was what,
and still is, bounces off the light. It might
be all the wire between us, messages
stacked up, masticating the new stitches,
the vine that inches up the light.
I wonder on the other side of things.
The moon, though, knows exactly where we are.
I hear my father, though tonight he brings

the fine sky down, battering the calendar.
Now is lying in my lap and I wish
clarity, that it were less standoffish.

3

The wreck. It is finally
that. It is not the moon or the word
messages. Between us the new stitches
glisten, and though it is hard,
it is father finally and the wire.
Between us the word falls between
clarity. I wonder about the cut,
about bent metal. I wonder about
the leaves that only last week still stood
still. Finally, the sky. It is not lying.
The wreckage of last week and the wreckage.
The knowing what was what already.
Of course the knowing. And the clarity,
an awful clarity, the slurred word "vine."

4

She said she wanted it to be right there.
She wanted water when the word said water,
not something that resembled it. A chair,
for instance. A long distance son or daughter.
Somebody shouting in the dream, go home,
the vine, the lip is bleeding and the wire
between you. And the what, the modicum
of which is also what. She wanted fire
right now because she was the match for her
desire. She wanted wreckage. She said go

back to your ready messages, the blur
of bad beginnings, the I am the broad flow.
Finally, something slurred about the lip,
abrupt messages, perhaps, the given slip.

5

The mathematization of nature,
brilliant wreckage, a bent
and rebent paperclip, soup
of disimaginings, sizzled wire.
He wanted to drive down into the ground,
grimy bank under which a flow of stone
would carry him, along which river slipped,
tossing cups and other sodden matter
backwards at the bindweed. He wanted the phone
dead, but it was too late to want. No one
came, no one cared
enough. It started, it, as the hurricane
inclined, started to un-
ravel, be there, be. Writhing and final.

6

I am walking through the dream's debris
counting Somalias. Acid rain
sizzles on the desert in Quebec, where three
Wilson's Phalaropes, somber as a pane
of glass, stand in stunned reflection.
Father is father, furious, his lip
lapped over by a thick pronunciation.
"Vine," says the voice in a slurred clip,
while two men lie on a bench somewhere, side

by gull, watchful even in sleep, their faces
pulled down, rachitic windowshade.
It is said we shall all change places
with the dirt, but it was dawn that cracked its gray yoke
over the stones and to the whole wreck woke.

Bowl of Soup

My father yells at the nurses.
Why not?
They bring him a bowl of soup.
A bowl of soup for a lifetime, he yells.
They tighten the straps.

One day in the mountains
the man who wrote "Melancholy Baby"
came for dinner.
He had a huge thing on his neck, a knob.
He told jokes and later died.

The nurses flip a coin
for who gets to go next.
It comes up tails.
Bring me a spoon, he yells.
A goddam straw.

Cardamom

for carrying the breath half
way, curry for the other.
Small spray of rattlenut. Cut-
leafed toothwort. Let the rain be
wind and the wind dissemble.
Put calla by the willow,
ditches by the roadside. Strew
comfrey and complaint, widow's
lament. The old gray goose goes
out like a starved owl. Meadow
of clammy everlasting
licks at the withered light. Heal-
all spills onto a carpet
of nails. Who is it gives back
what he was given? Who goes
back to the desolate core?
Here, take it. Blind pencil
in a blind cup and a laugh
like cinnamon azimuth.
Something that has no name, no
way to determine the dirt
or take up the slack in rock.
Calyx of dwindling hours,
uncertain cup of a thin
unscented blossom, open
your snow, put on your brief scarf.

Scaly Flank

I do not know how to tell you this
without breaking glass. Clearly,
you have poured your life's joys
and terrors into these shapely forms.
There they stand, a testament to the skill
you have mastered and the persuasive
power of those who convinced you
that mastery of them was important.
What can I say? You have done
what you have done lovingly.
You have looked into every corner
of this house. You have run your hands
along its seams and imperfections.
Surely, you say, something must come of this.

And it will. But it will come first
as a kind of death, standing up.
Everything you have brought with you
will need to be taken back. Nothing
you have done thus far will survive.
You will not survive, for the redoing
of what you have done will require
a new person. You will feel this person inside you,
but you will cling to the old one.
He will drag you back, saying
"Stay here where the milky light
empties across the floor."
And you will draw back, preferring
the company of old friends, shapely forms.

You will do this a long time. You may
do this forever, reaching cautiously
out, touching the strange flesh,
and turning away, and knowing from what,
but turning anyway, and saying to someone
beside you, someone in the next room,
maybe no one, "I have touched it now,
I have touched the strange flesh,
isn't that enough, can I go now,
can I go," and the someone or no one
saying just what you want them to,
just what you were afraid they might:
Yes, of course, go, go back.

And you go back to the old fork,
to the horse and barn, go back
to the scream at night, to the room,
the one above the warehouse, go back
to the days you threw down the stairs,
poured like dirt into the water,
days when you knew nothing
in the morning and the same late at night
or early the next star-crusted morning
when you could no longer keep yourself
awake and so dropped where you stood
and slept, so deeply you forgot
that you knew nothing and were nothing
and woke witless to a new day.

Try to remember that day,
the hills in back of the house.
Imagine waking up in a ditch,
the sun just touching the tips
of the trees in the distance.
You've done what you've done. It's over.
It was good, it was OK, and it's over.
Lie there and let it run out of you.
Let the sun slide down the length of your body.
Let the shapeliness and the fear go.
Worms are tugging at your flesh.
Whatever you're thinking now,
follow it. No matter how strange,
place your hand on the scaly flank.

Roger Mitchell is the author of four other books of poetry, including *Adirondack*, also published by BkMk Press. His poetry has won a number of awards, including the Midland Poetry Award, a Borestone Mountain Award, a Chester H. Jones Award, an NEA fellowship, and a fellowship from the Indiana Arts Commission. His book of non-fiction, *Clear Pond: The Reconstruction of a Life*, published by Syracuse University Press, won the John Ben Snow Award. He has been an editor, a reviewer, and an essayist. He teaches in the English department at Indiana University where he was for many years director of the creative writing program.